THE PSYCHOLOGY OF ERRORS

A GENERAL INTRODUCTION TO PSYCHOANALYSIS

SIGMUND FREUD

Translated by
G. STANLEY HALL

CONTENTS

INTRODUCTION   1
I   17
II   41
III   72

INTRODUCTION

I DO not know how familiar some of you may be, either from your reading or from hearsay, with psychoanalysis. But, in keeping with the title of these lectures—*A General Introduction to Psychoanalysis*—I am obliged to proceed as though you knew nothing about this subject, and stood in need of preliminary instruction.

To be sure, this much I may presume that you do know, namely, that psychoanalysis is a method of treating nervous patients medically. And just at this point I can give you an example to illustrate how the procedure in this field is precisely the reverse of that which is the rule in medicine. Usually when we introduce a patient to a medical technique which is strange to him we minimize its difficulties and give him confident promises concerning the result of the treatment. When, however, we undertake psychoanalytic treatment with a neurotic patient we proceed differently. We hold before him the difficulties of the method, its length, the exertions and the sacrifices which it will cost him; and, as to the result, we tell him that we make no definite promises, that the result depends on his conduct, on his understanding, on his adaptability, on his perseverance. We have, of course, excellent motives for conduct which seems so perverse, and into which you will perhaps gain insight at a later point in these lectures.

Do not be offended, therefore, if, for the present, I treat you as I treat these neurotic patients. Frankly, I shall dissuade you from coming to hear me a second time. With this intention I shall show what imperfections are necessarily involved in the teaching of psychoanalysis and what difficulties stand in the way of gaining a personal judgment. I shall show you how the whole trend of your previous training and all your accustomed mental habits must unavoidably have made you opponents of psychoanalysis, and how much you must overcome in yourselves in order to master this instinctive opposition. Of course I cannot predict how much psychoanalytic understanding you will gain from my lectures, but I can promise this, that by listening to them you will not learn how to undertake a psychoanalytic treatment or how to carry one to completion. Furthermore, should I find anyone among you who does not feel satisfied with a cursory acquaintance with psychoanalysis, but who would like to enter into a more enduring relationship with it, I shall not only dissuade him, but I shall actually warn him against it. As things now stand, a person would, by such a choice of profession, ruin his every chance of success at a university, and if he goes out into the world as a practicing physician, he will find himself in a society which does not understand his aims, which regards him with suspicion and hostility, and which turns loose upon him all the malicious spirits which lurk within it.

However, there are always enough individuals who are interested in anything which may be added to the sum total of knowledge, despite such inconveniences. Should there be any of this type among you, and should they ignore my dissuasion and return to the next of these lectures, they will be welcome. But all of you have the right to know what these difficulties of psychoanalysis are to which I have alluded.

First of all, we encounter the difficulties inherent in the teaching and exposition of psychoanalysis. In your medical instruction you have been accustomed to visual demonstration. You see the anatomical specimen, the precipitate in the chemical reaction, the contraction of the muscle as the result of the stimulation of its nerves. Later the patient is presented to your senses; the symptoms of his malady, the products of the pathological processes, in many cases even the cause of the disease is shown in isolated state. In the surgical department you are made to witness the steps by which one brings relief to the patient, and are permitted to attempt to practice them. Even in psychiatry, the demonstration affords you, by the patient's changed facial play, his manner of speech and his behavior, a wealth of observations which leave far-reaching impressions. Thus the medical teacher preponderantly plays the role of a guide and instructor who accompanies you through a museum in which you contract an immediate relationship to the exhibits, and in which you believe yourself to have been convinced through your own observation of the existence of the new things you see.

Unfortunately, everything is different in psychoanalysis. In psychoanalysis nothing occurs but the interchange of words between the patient and the physician. The patient talks, tells of his past experiences and present impressions, complains, confesses his wishes and emotions. The physician listens, tries to direct the thought processes of the patient, reminds him of things, forces his attention into certain channels, gives him explanations and observes the reactions of understanding or denial which he calls forth in the patient. The uneducated relatives of our patients—persons who are impressed only by the visible and tangible, preferably by such procedure as one sees in the moving picture theatres—never miss an opportunity of voicing their scepticism as to how one can "do anything for the malady through mere talk." Such thinking, of course, is as shortsighted as it is inconsistent. For these are the very persons who know with such certainty that the patients "merely imagine" their symptoms. Words were originally magic, and the word retains much of its old magical power even to-day. With words one man can make another blessed, or drive him to despair; by words the teacher transfers his knowledge to the pupil; by words the speaker sweeps his audience with him and determines its judgments and decisions. Words call forth effects and are the universal means of influencing human beings. Therefore let us not underestimate the use of words in psychotherapy, and let us be satisfied if we may be auditors of the words which are exchanged between the analyst and his patient.

But even that is impossible. The conversation

of which the psychoanalytic treatment consists brooks no auditor, it cannot be demonstrated. One can, of course, present a neurasthenic or hysteric to the students in a psychiatric lecture. He tells of his complaints and symptoms, but of nothing else. The communications which are necessary for the analysis are made only under the conditions of a special affective relationship to the physician; the patient would become dumb as soon as he became aware of a single impartial witness. For these communications concern the most intimate part of his psychic life, everything which as a socially independent person he must conceal from others; these communications deal with everything which, as a harmonious personality, he will not admit even to himself.

You cannot, therefore, "listen in" on a psychoanalytic treatment. You can only hear of it. You will get to know psychoanalysis, in the strictest sense of the word, only by hearsay. Such instruction even at second hand, will place you in quite an unusual position for forming a judgment. For it is obvious that everything depends on the faith you are able to put in the instructor.

Imagine that you are not attending a psychiatric, but an historical lecture, and that the lecturer is telling you about the life and martial deeds of Alexander the Great. What would be your reasons for believing in the authenticity of his statements?

At first sight, the condition of affairs seems even more unfavorable than in the case of psychoanalysis, for the history professor was as little a participant in Alexander's campaigns as you were; the psychoanalyst at least tells you of things in connection with which he himself has played some role. But then the question turns on this—what set of facts can the historian marshal in support of his position? He can refer you to the accounts of ancient authors, who were either contemporaries themselves, or who were at least closer to the events in question; that is, he will refer you to the books of Diodor, Plutarch, Arrian, etc. He can place before you pictures of the preserved coins and statues of the king and can pass down your rows a photograph of the Pompeiian mosaics of the battle of Issos. Yet, strictly speaking, all these documents prove only that previous generations already believed in Alexander's existence and in the reality of his deeds, and your criticism might begin anew at this point. You will then find that not everything recounted of Alexander is credible, or capable of proof in detail; yet even then I cannot believe that you will leave the lecture hall a disbeliever in the reality of Alexander the Great. Your decision will be determined chiefly by two considerations; firstly, that the lecturer has no conceivable motive for presenting as truth something which he does not himself believe to be true, and secondly, that all available histories present the events in approximately the same manner. If you then proceed to the verification of the older sources, you will consider the same data, the possible motives of the writers and the consistency of the various parts of the evidence. The result of the examination will surely be convincing in the case of Alexander. It will probably turn out differently when applied to individuals like Moses and Nimrod. But what doubts you might raise against the credibility of the psychoanalytic reporter you will see plainly enough upon a later occasion.

At this point you have a right to raise the question, "If there is no such thing as objective verification of psychoanalysis, and no possibility of demonstrating it, how can one possibly learn psychoanalysis and convince himself of the truth of its claims?" The fact is, the study is not easy and there are not many persons who have learned psychoanalysis thoroughly; but nevertheless, there is a feasible way. Psychoanalysis is learned, first of all, from a study of one's self, through the study of one's own personality. This is not quite what is ordinarily called self-observation, but, at a pinch, one can sum it up thus. There is a whole series of very common and universally known psychic phenomena, which, after some instruction in the technique of psychoanalysis, one can make the subject matter of analysis in one's self. By so doing one obtains the desired conviction of the reality of the occurrences which psychoanalysis describes and of the correctness of its fundamental conception. To be sure, there are definite limits imposed on progress by this method. One gets much further if one allows himself to be analyzed by a competent analyst, observes the effect of the analysis on his own ego, and at the same time makes use of the opportunity to become familiar with the finer details of the technique of procedure. This excellent method is, of course, only practicable for one person, never for an entire class.

There is a second difficulty in your relation to psychoanalysis for which I cannot hold the science itself responsible, but for which I must ask you to take the responsibility upon yourselves, ladies and gentlemen, at least in so far as you have hitherto pursued medical studies. Your previous training has given your mental activity a definite bent which leads you far away from psychoanalysis. You have been trained to reduce the functions of an organism and its disorders anatomically, to explain them in terms of chemistry and physics and to conceive them biologically, but no portion of your interest has been directed to the psychic life, in which, after all, the activity of this wonderfully complex organism culminates. For this reason psychological thinking has remained strange to you and you have accustomed yourselves to regard it with suspicion, to deny it the character of the scientific, to leave it to the laymen, poets, natural philosophers and mystics. Such a delimitation is surely harmful to your medical activity, for the patient will, as is usual in all human relationships, confront you first of all with his psychic facade; and I am afraid your penalty will be this, that you will be forced to relinquish a portion of the therapeutic influence to which you aspire, to those lay physicians, nature-cure fakers and mystics whom you despise.

I am not overlooking the excuse, whose existence one must admit, for this deficiency in your previous training. There is no philosophical science of therapy which could be made practicable for your medical purpose. Neither speculative philosophy nor descriptive psychology nor that so-called experimental psychology which allies itself with the physiology of the sense organs as it is taught in the schools, is in a position to teach you anything useful concerning the relation between the physical and the psychical or to put into your hand the key to the understanding of a possible disorder of the psychic functions. Within the field of medicine, psychiatry does, it is true, occupy itself with the description of the observed psychic disorders and with their grouping into clinical symptom-pictures; but in their better hours the psychiatrists themselves doubt whether their purely descriptive account deserves the name of a science. The symptoms which constitute these clinical pictures are known neither in their origin, in their mechanism, nor in their mutual relationship. There are either no discoverable corresponding changes of the anatomical organ of the soul, or else the changes are of such a nature as to yield no enlightenment. Such psychic disturbances are open to therapeutic influence only when they can be identified as secondary phenomena of an otherwise organic affection.

Here is the gap which psychoanalysis aims to fill. It prepares to give psychiatry the omitted psychological foundation, it hopes to reveal the common basis from which, as a starting point, constant correlation of bodily and psychic disturbances becomes comprehensible. To this end, it must divorce itself from every anatomical, chemical or physiological supposition which is alien to it. It must work throughout with purely psychological therapeutic concepts, and just for that reason I fear that it will at first seem strange to you.

I will not make you, your previous training, or your mental bias share the guilt of the next difficulty. With two of its assertions, psychoanalysis offends the whole world and draws aversion upon itself. One of these assertions offends an intellectual prejudice, the other an aesthetic-moral one. Let us not think too lightly of these prejudices; they are powerful things, remnants of useful, even necessary, developments of mankind. They are retained through powerful affects, and the battle against them is a hard one.

The first of these displeasing assertions of psychoanalysis is this, that the psychic processes are in themselves unconscious, and that those which are conscious are merely isolated acts and parts of the total psychic life. Recollect that we are, on the contrary, accustomed to identify the psychic with the conscious. Consciousness actually means for us the distinguishing characteristic of the psychic life, and psychology is the science of the content of consciousness. Indeed, so obvious does this identification seem to us that we consider its slightest contradiction obvious nonsense, and yet psychoanalysis cannot avoid raising this contradiction; it cannot accept the identity of the conscious with the psychic. Its definition of the psychic affirms that they are processes of the nature of feeling, thinking, willing; and it must assert that there is such a thing as unconscious thinking and unconscious willing. But with this assertion psychoanalysis has alienated, to start with, the sympathy of all friends of sober science, and has laid itself open to the suspicion of being a fantastic mystery study which would build in darkness and fish in murky waters. You, however, ladies and gentlemen, naturally cannot as yet understand what justification I have for stigmatizing as a prejudice so abstract a phrase as this one, that "the psychic is consciousness." You cannot know what evaluation can have led to the denial of the unconscious, if such a thing really exists, and what advantage may have resulted from this denial. It sounds like a mere argument over words whether one shall say that the psychic coincides with the conscious or whether one shall extend it beyond that, and yet I can assure you that by the acceptance of unconscious processes you have paved the way for a decisively new orientation in the world and in science.

Just as little can you guess how intimate a connection this initial boldness of psychoanalysis has with the one which follows. The next assertion which psychoanalysis proclaims as one of its discoveries, affirms that those instinctive impulses which one can only call sexual in the narrower as well as in the wider sense, play an uncommonly large role in the causation of nervous and mental diseases, and that those impulses are a causation which has never been adequately appreciated. Nay, indeed, psychoanalysis claims that these same sexual impulses have made contributions whose value cannot be overestimated to the highest cultural, artistic and social achievements of the human mind.

According to my experience, the aversion to this conclusion of psychoanalysis is the most significant source of the opposition which it encounters. Would you like to know how we explain this fact? We believe that civilization was forged by the driving force of vital necessity, at the cost of instinct-satisfaction, and that the process is to a large extent constantly repeated anew, since each individual who newly enters the human community repeats the sacrifices of his instinct-satisfaction for the sake of the common good. Among the instinctive forces thus utilized, the sexual impulses play a significant role. They are thereby sublimated, i.e., they are diverted from their sexual goals and directed to ends socially higher and no longer sexual. But this result is unstable. The sexual instincts are poorly tamed. Each individual who wishes to ally himself with the achievements of civilization is exposed to the danger of having his sexual instincts rebel against this sublimation. Society can conceive of no more serious menace to its civilization than would arise through the satisfying of the sexual instincts by their redirection toward their original goals. Society, therefore, does not relish being reminded of this ticklish spot in its origin; it has no interest in having the strength of the sexual instincts recognized and the meaning of the sexual life to the individual clearly delineated. On the contrary, society has taken the course of diverting attention from this whole field. This is the reason why society will not tolerate the above-mentioned results of psychoanalytic research, and would prefer to brand it as aesthetically offensive and morally objectionable or dangerous. Since, however, one cannot attack an ostensibly objective result of scientific inquiry with such objections, the criticism must be translated to an intellectual level if it is to be voiced. But it is a predisposition of human nature to consider an unpleasant idea untrue, and then it is easy to find arguments against it. Society thus brands what is unpleasant as untrue, denying the conclusions of psychoanalysis with logical and pertinent arguments. These arguments originate from affective sources, however, and society holds to these prejudices against all attempts at refutation.

However, we may claim, ladies and gentlemen, that we have followed no bias of any sort in making any of these contested statements. We merely wished to state facts which we believe to have been discovered by toilsome labor. And we now claim the right unconditionally to reject the interference in scientific research of any such practical considerations, even before we have investigated whether the apprehension which these considerations are meant to instil are justified or not.

These, therefore, are but a few of the difficulties which stand in the way of your occupation with psychoanalysis. They are perhaps more than enough for a beginning. If you can overcome their deterrent impression, we shall continue.

I

WE begin with an investigation, not with hypotheses. To this end we choose certain phenomena which are very frequent, very familiar and very little heeded, and which have nothing to do with the pathological, inasmuch as they can be observed in every normal person. I refer to the errors which an individual commits—as for example, errors of speech in which he wishes to say something and uses the wrong word; or those which happen to him in writing, and which he may or may not notice; or the case of misreading, in which one reads in the print or writing something different from what is actually there. A similar phenomenon occurs in those cases of mishearing what is said to one, where there is no question of an organic disturbance of the auditory function. Another series of such occurrences is based on forgetfulness—but on a forgetfulness which is not permanent, but temporary, as for instance when one cannot think of a name which one knows and always recognizes; or when one forgets to carry out a project at the proper time but which one remembers again later, and therefore has only forgotten for a certain interval. In a third class this characteristic of transience is lacking, as for example in mislaying things so that they cannot be found again, or in the analogous case of losing things. Here we are dealing with a kind of forgetfulness to which one reacts differently from the other cases, a forgetfulness at which one is surprised and annoyed, instead of considering it comprehensible. Allied with these phenomena is that of erroneous ideas—in which the element of transience is again prominent, inasmuch as for a while one believes something which, before and after that time, one knows to be untrue—and a number of similar phenomena of different designations.

These are all occurrences whose inner connection is expressed in the use of the same prefix of designation.[1] They are almost all unimportant, generally temporary and without much significance in the life of the individual. It is only rarely that one of them, such as the phenomenon of losing things, attains to a certain practical importance. For that reason also they do not attract much attention, they arouse only weak affects.

It is, therefore, to these phenomena that I would now direct your attention. But you will object, with annoyance: "There are so many sublime riddles in the external world, just as there are in the narrower world of the psychic life, and so many wonders in the field of psychic disturbances which demand and deserve elucidation, that it really seems frivolous to waste labor and interest on such trifles. If you can explain to us how an individual with sound eyes and ears can, in broad daylight, see and hear things that do not exist, or why another individual suddenly believes himself persecuted by those whom up to that time he loved best, or defend, with the most ingenious arguments, delusions which must seem nonsense to any child, then we will be willing to consider psychoanalysis seriously. But if psychoanalysis can do nothing better than to occupy us with the question of why a speaker used the wrong word, or why a housekeeper mislaid her keys, or such trifles, then we know something better to do with our time and interest."

My reply is: "Patience, ladies and gentlemen. I think your criticism is not on the right track. It is true that psychoanalysis cannot boast that it has never occupied itself with trifles. On the contrary, the objects of its observations are generally those simple occurrences which the other sciences have thrown aside as much too insignificant, the waste products of the phenomenal world. But are you not confounding, in your criticism, the sublimity of the problems with the conspicuousness of their manifestations? Are there not very important things which under certain circumstances, and at certain times, can betray themselves only by very faint signs? I could easily cite a great many instances of this kind. From what vague signs, for instance, do the young gentlemen of this audience conclude that they have won the favor of a lady? Do you await an explicit declaration, an ardent embrace, or does not a glance, scarcely perceptible to others, a fleeting gesture, the prolonging of a hand-shake by one second, suffice? And if you are a criminal lawyer, and engaged in the investigation of a murder, do you actually expect the murderer to leave his photograph and address on the scene of the crime, or would you, of necessity, content yourself with fainter and less certain traces of that individual? Therefore, let us not undervalue small signs; perhaps by means of them we will succeed in getting on the track of greater things. I agree with you that the larger problems of the world and of science have the first claim on our interest. But it is generally of little avail to form the definite resolution to devote oneself to the investigation of this or that problem. Often one does not know in which direction to take the next step. In scientific research it is more fruitful to attempt what happens to be before one at the moment and for whose investigation there is a discoverable method. If one does that thoroughly without prejudice or predisposition, one may, with good fortune, and by virtue of the connection which links each thing to every other (hence also the small to the great) discover even from such modest research a point of approach to the study of the big problems."

Thus would I answer, in order to secure your attention for the consideration of these apparently insignificant errors made by normal people. At this point, we will question a stranger to psychoanalysis and ask him how he explains these occurrences.

His first answer is sure to be, "Oh, they are not worth an explanation; they are merely slight accidents." What does he mean by this? Does he mean to assert that there are any occurrences so insignificant that they fall out of the causal sequence of things, or that they might just as well be something different from what they are? If any one thus denies the determination of natural phenomena at one such point, he has vitiated the entire scientific viewpoint. One can then point out to him how much more consistent is the religious point of view, when it explicitly asserts that "No sparrow falls from the roof without God's special wish." I imagine our friend will not be willing to follow his first answer to its logical conclusion; he will interrupt and say that if he were to study these things he would probably find an explanation for them. He will say that this is a case of slight functional disturbance, of an inaccurate psychic act whose causal factors can be outlined. A man who otherwise speaks correctly may make a slip of the tongue—when he is slightly ill or fatigued; when he is excited; when his attention is concentrated on something else. It is easy to prove these statements. Slips of the tongue do really occur with special frequency when one is tired, when one has a headache or when one is indisposed. Forgetting proper names is a very frequent occurrence under these circumstances. Many persons even recognize the imminence of an indisposition by the inability to recall proper names. Often also one mixes up words or objects during excitement, one picks up the wrong things; and the forgetting of projects, as well as the doing of any number of other unintentional acts, becomes conspicuous when one is distracted; in other words, when one's attention is concentrated on other things. A familiar instance of such distraction is the professor in *Fliegende Blätter*, who takes the wrong hat because he is thinking of the problems which he wishes to treat in his next book.

Each of us knows from experience some examples of how one can forget projects which one has planned and promises which one has made, because an experience has intervened which has preoccupied one deeply.

This seems both comprehensible and irrefutable. It is perhaps not very interesting, not as we expected it to be. But let us consider this explanation of errors. The conditions which have been cited as necessary for the occurrence of these phenomena are not all identical. Illness and disorders of circulation afford a physiological basis. Excitement, fatigue and distraction are conditions of a different sort, which one could designate as psycho-physiological. About these latter it is easy to theorize. Fatigue, as well as distraction, and perhaps also general excitement, cause a scattering of the attention which can result in the act in progress not receiving sufficient attention. This act can then be more easily interrupted than usual, and may be inexactly carried out. A slight illness, or a change in the distribution of blood in the central organ of the nervous system, can have the same effect, inasmuch as it influences the determining factor, the distribution of attention, in a similar way. In all cases, therefore, it is a question of the effects of a distraction of the attention, caused either by organic or psychic factors.

But this does not seem to yield much of interest for our psychoanalytic investigation. We might even feel tempted to give up the subject. To be sure, when we look more closely we find that not everything squares with this attention theory of psychological errors, or that at any rate not everything can be directly deduced from it. We find that such errors and such forgetting occur even when people are not fatigued, distracted or excited, but are in every way in their normal state; unless, in consequence of these errors, one were to attribute to them an excitement which they themselves do not acknowledge. Nor is the mechanism so simple that the success of an act is assured by an intensification of the attention bestowed upon it, and endangered by its diminution. There are many acts which one performs in a purely automatic way and with very little attention, but which are yet carried out quite successfully. The pedestrian who scarcely knows where he is going, nevertheless keeps to the right road and stops at his destination without having gone astray. At least, this is the rule. The practiced pianist touches the right keys without thinking of them. He may, of course, also make an occasional mistake, but if automatic playing increased the likelihood of errors, it would be just the virtuoso whose playing has, through practice, become most automatic, who would be the most exposed to this danger. Yet we see, on the contrary, that many acts are most successfully carried out when they are not the objects of particularly concentrated attention, and that the mistakes occur just at the point where one is most anxious to be accurate—where a distraction of the necessary attention is therefore surely least permissible. One could then say that this is the effect of the "excitement," but we do not understand why the excitement does not intensify the concentration of attention on the goal that is so much desired. If in an important speech or discussion anyone says the opposite of what he means, then that can hardly be explained according to the psycho-physiological or the attention theories.

There are also many other small phenomena accompanying these errors, which are not understood and which have not been rendered comprehensible to us by these explanations. For instance, when one has temporarily forgotten a name, one is annoyed, one is determined to recall it and is unable to give up the attempt. Why is it that despite his annoyance the individual cannot succeed, as he wishes, in directing his attention to the word which is "on the tip of his tongue," and which he instantly recognizes when it is pronounced to him? Or, to take another example, there are cases in which the errors multiply, link themselves together, substitute for each other. The first time one forgets an appointment; the next time, after having made a special resolution not to forget it, one discovers that one has made a mistake in the day or hour. Or one tries by devious means to remember a forgotten word, and in the course of so doing loses track of a second name which would have been of use in finding the first. If one then pursues this second name, a third gets lost, and so on. It is notorious that the same thing can happen in the case of misprints, which are of course to be considered as errors of the typesetter. A stubborn error of this sort is said to have crept into a Social-Democratic paper, where, in the account of a certain festivity was printed, "Among those present was His Highness, the Clown Prince." The next day a correction was attempted. The paper apologized and said, "The sentence should, of course, have read 'The Clown Prince.'" One likes to attribute these occurrences to the printer's devil, to the goblin of the typesetting machine, and the like—figurative expressions which at least go beyond a psycho-physiological theory of the misprint.

I do not know if you are acquainted with the fact that one can provoke slips of the tongue, can call them forth by suggestion, as it were. An anecdote will serve to illustrate this. Once when a novice on the stage was entrusted with the important role in *The Maid of Orleans* of announcing to the King, "Connétable sheathes his sword," the star played the joke of repeating to the frightened beginner during the rehearsal, instead of the text, the following, "Comfortable sends back his steed,"[2] and he attained his end. In the performance the unfortunate actor actually made his début with this distorted announcement; even after he had been amply warned against so doing, or perhaps just for that reason.

These little characteristics of errors are not exactly illuminated by the theory of diverted attention. But that does not necessarily prove the whole theory wrong. There is perhaps something missing, a complement by the addition of which the theory would be made completely satisfactory. But many of the errors themselves can be regarded from another aspect.

Let us select slips of the tongue, as best suited to our purposes. We might equally well choose slips of the pen or of reading. But at this point, we must make clear to ourselves the fact that so far we have inquired only as to when and under what conditions one's tongue slips, and have received an answer on this point only. One can, however, direct one's interest elsewhere and ask why one makes just this particular slip and no other; one can consider what the slip results in. You must realize that as long as one does not answer this question—does not explain the effect produced by the slip—the phenomenon in its psychological aspect remains an accident, even if its physiological explanation has been found. When it happens that I commit a slip of the tongue, I could obviously make any one of an infinite number of slips, and in place of the one right word say any one of a thousand others, make innumerable distortions of the right word. Now, is there anything which forces upon me in a specific instance just this one special slip out of all those which are possible, or does that remain accidental and arbitrary, and can nothing rational be found in answer to this question?

Two authors, Meringer and Mayer (a philologist and a psychiatrist) did indeed in 1895 make the attempt to approach the problem of slips of the tongue from this side. They collected examples and first treated them from a purely descriptive standpoint. That, of course, does not yet furnish any explanation, but may open the way to one. They differentiated the distortions which the intended phrase suffered through the slip, into: interchanges of positions of words, interchanges of parts of words, perseverations, compoundings and substitutions. I will give you examples of these authors' main categories. It is a case of interchange of the first sort if someone says "the Milo of Venus" instead of "the Venus of Milo." An example of the second type of interchange, "I had a blush of rood to the head" instead of "rush of blood"; a perseveration would be the familiar misplaced toast, "I ask you to join me in hiccoughing the health of our chief."[3] These three forms of slips are not very frequent. You will find those cases much more frequent in which the slip results from a drawing together or compounding of syllables; for example, a gentleman on the street addresses a lady with the words, "If you will allow me, madame, I should be very glad to *inscort* you."[4] In the compounded word there is obviously besides the word "escort," also the word "insult" (and parenthetically we may remark that the young man will not find much favor with the lady). As an example of the substitution, Meringer and Mayer cite the following: "A man says, 'I put the specimens in the letterbox,' instead of 'in the hot-bed,' and the like."[5]

The explanation which the two authors attempt to formulate on the basis of this collection of examples is peculiarly inadequate. They hold that the sounds and syllables of words have different values, and that the production and perception of more highly valued syllables can interfere with those of lower values. They obviously base this conclusion on the cases of fore-sounding and perseveration which are not at all frequent; in other cases of slips of the tongue the question of such sound priorities, if any exist, does not enter at all. The most frequent cases of slips of the tongue are those in which instead of a certain word one says another which resembles it; and one may consider this resemblance sufficient explanation. For example, a professor says in his initial lecture, "I am not *inclined* to evaluate the merits of my predecessor."[6] Or another professor says, "In the case of the female genital, despite many *temptations* ... I mean many attempts ... etc."[7]

The most common, and also the most conspicuous form of slips of the tongue, however, is that of saying the exact opposite of what one meant to say. In such cases, one goes far afield from the problem of sound relations and resemblance effects, and can cite, instead of these, the fact that opposites have an obviously close relationship to each other, and have particularly close relations in the psychology of association. There are historical examples of this sort. A president of our House of Representatives once opened the assembly with the words, "Gentlemen, I declare a quorum present, and herewith declare the assembly *closed*."

Similar, in its trickiness, to the relation of opposites is the effect of any other facile association which may under certain circumstances arise most inopportunely. Thus, for instance, there is the story which relates that on the occasion of a festivity in honor of the marriage of a child of H. Helmholtz with a child of the well-known discoverer and captain of industry, W. Siemon, the famous physiologist Dubois-Reymond was asked to speak. He concluded his undoubtedly sparkling toast with the words, "Success to the new firm—Siemens and—Halski!" That, of course, was the name of the well-known old firm. The association of the two names must have been about as easy for a native of Berlin as "Weber and Fields" to an American.

Thus we must add to the sound relations and word resemblances the influence of word associations. But that is not all. In a series of cases, an explanation of the observed slip is unsuccessful unless we take into account what phrase had been said or even thought previously. This again makes it a case of perseveration of the sort stressed by Meringer, but of a longer duration. I must admit, I am on the whole of the impression that we are further than ever from an explanation of slips of the tongue!

However, I hope I am not wrong when I say that during the above investigation of these examples of slips of the tongue, we have all obtained a new impression on which it will be of value to dwell. We sought the general conditions under which slips of the tongue occur, and then the influences which determine the kind of distortion resulting from the slip, but we have in no way yet considered the effect of the slip of the tongue in itself, without regard to its origin. And if we should decide to do so we must finally have the courage to assert, "In some of the examples cited, the product of the slip also makes sense." What do we mean by "it makes sense"? It means, I think, that the product of the slip has itself a right to be considered as a valid psychic act which also has its purpose, as a manifestation having content and meaning. Hitherto we have always spoken of errors, but now it seems as if sometimes the error itself were quite a normal act, except that it has thrust itself into the place of some other expected or intended act.

In isolated cases this valid meaning seems obvious and unmistakable. When the president with his opening words closes the session of the House of Representatives, instead of opening it, we are inclined to consider this error meaningful by reason of our knowledge of the circumstances under which the slip occurred. He expects no good of the assembly, and would be glad if he could terminate it immediately. The pointing out of this meaning, the interpretation of this error, gives us no difficulty. Or a lady, pretending to admire, says to another, "I am sure you must have messed up this charming hat yourself."[8] No scientific quibbles in the world can keep us from discovering in this slip the idea "this hat is a mess." Or a lady who is known for her energetic disposition, relates, "My husband asked the doctor to what diet he should keep. But the doctor said he didn't need any diet, he should eat and drink whatever *I* want." This slip of tongue is quite an unmistakable expression of a consistent purpose.

Ladies and gentlemen, if it should turn out that not only a few cases of slips of the tongue and of errors in general, but the larger part of them, have a meaning, then this meaning of errors of which we have hitherto made no mention, will unavoidably become of the greatest interest to us and will, with justice, force all other points of view into the background. We could then ignore all physiological and psycho-physiological conditions and devote ourselves to the purely psychological investigations of the sense, that is, the meaning, the purpose of these errors. To this end therefore we will not fail, shortly, to study a more extensive compilation of material.

But before we undertake this task, I should like to invite you to follow another line of thought with me. It has repeatedly happened that a poet has made use of slips of the tongue or some other error as a means of poetic presentation. This fact in itself must prove to us that he considers the error, the slip of the tongue for instance, as meaningful; for he creates it on purpose, and it is not a case of the poet committing an accidental slip of the pen and then letting his pen-slip stand as a tongue-slip of his character. He wants to make something clear to us by this slip of the tongue, and we may examine what it is, whether he wishes to indicate by this that the person in question is distracted or fatigued. Of course, we do not wish to exaggerate the importance of the fact that the poet did make use of a slip to express his meaning. It could nevertheless really be a psychic accident, or meaningful only in very rare cases, and the poet would still retain the right to infuse it with meaning through his setting. As to their poetic use, however, it would not be surprising if we should glean more information concerning slips of the tongue from the poet than from the philologist or the psychiatrist.

Such an example of a slip of the tongue occurs in *Wallenstein* (*Piccolomini*, Act 1, Scene 5). In the previous scene, Max Piccolomini has most passionately sided with the Herzog, and dilated ardently on the blessings of peace which disclosed themselves to him during the trip on which he accompanied Wallenstein's daughter to the camp. He leaves his father and the courtier, Questenberg, plunged in deepest consternation. And then the fifth scene continues:
Q.

> *Alas! Alas! and stands it so?*
> *What friend! and do we let him go away*
> *In this delusion—let him go away?*

> Not call him back immediately,
>   not open
> His eyes upon the spot?

OCTAVIO.

> (Recovering himself out of a deep
>   study)
> He has now opened mine,
> And I see more than pleases me.

Q.

>   What is it?

OCTAVIO.

>   A curse on this journey!

Q.

>   But why so? What is it?

OCTAVIO.

> Come, come along, friend! I must
>   follow up
> The ominous track immediately.
>   Mine eyes

Are opened now, and I must use them.
    Come!
(Draws Q. on with him.)

Q.

What now? Where go you then?

OCTAVIO.

(Hastily.) *To* her *herself*

Q.

To—

OCTAVIO.

(Interrupting him and correcting
    himself.)
To the duke. Come, let us go—.

Octavio meant to say, "To him, to the lord," but his tongue slips and through his words "*to her*" he betrays to us, at least, the fact that he had quite clearly recognized the influence which makes the young war hero dream of peace.

A still more impressive example was found by O. Rank in Shakespeare. It occurs in the *Merchant of Venice,* in the famous scene in which the fortunate suitor makes his choice among the three caskets; and perhaps I can do no better than to read to you here Rank's short account of the incident:

"A slip of the tongue which occurs in Shakespeare's *Merchant of Venice,* Act III, Scene II, is exceedingly delicate in its poetic motivation and technically brilliant in its handling. Like the slip in *Wallenstein* quoted by Freud (*Psychopathology of Everyday Life,* 2d ed., p. 48), it shows that the poets well know the meaning of these errors and assume their comprehensibility to the audience. Portia, who by her father's wish has been bound to the choice of a husband by lot, has so far escaped all her unfavored suitors through the fortunes of chance. Since she has finally found in Bassanio the suitor to whom she is attached, she fears that he, too, will choose the wrong casket. She would like to tell him that even in that event he may rest assured of her love, but is prevented from so doing by her oath. In this inner conflict the poet makes her say to the welcome suitor:

PORTIA:

> *I pray you tarry; pause a day or two,*
> *Before you hazard; for, in choosing*
>   *wrong*
> *I lose your company; therefore, forbear a*
>   *while:*

> *There's something tells me, (but it is not*
>   *love)*
> *I would not lose you:* * * *
> * * * *I could teach you*
> *How to choose right, but then I am*
>   *forsworn,*
> *So will I never be: so may you miss me;*
> *But if you do, you'll make me wish a sin*
> *That I had been forsworn. Beshrew your*
>   *eyes.*
> *They have o'erlook'd me, and*
>   *divided me;*
> *One half of me is yours, the other half*
>   *yours,*
> *Mine own, I would say: but if mine,*
>   *then yours,*
> *And so all yours.*

Just that, therefore, which she meant merely to indicate faintly to him or really to conceal from him entirely, namely that even before the choice of the lot she was his and loved him, this the poet—with admirable psychological delicacy of feeling—makes apparent by her slip; and is able, by this artistic device, to quiet the unbearable uncertainty of the lover, as well as the equal suspense of the audience as to the issue of the choice."

Notice, at the end, how subtly Portia reconciles the two declarations which are contained in the slip, how she resolves the contradiction between them and finally still manages to keep her promise:

> "* * * but if mine, then yours,
> And so all yours."

Another thinker, alien to the field of medicine, accidentally disclosed the meaning of errors by an observation which has anticipated our attempts at explanation. You all know the clever satires of Lichtenberg (1742-1749), of which Goethe said, "Where he jokes, there lurks a problem concealed." Not infrequently the joke also brings to light the solution of the problem. Lichtenberg mentions in his jokes and satiric comments the remark that he always read "Agamemnon" for "angenommen,"[9] so intently had he read Homer. Herein is really contained the whole theory of misreadings.

At the next session we will see whether we can agree with the poets in their conception of the meaning of psychological errors.

---

1. "Fehl-leistungen."
2. In the German, the correct announcement is, "Connetable schickt sein Schwert zurück." The novice, as a result of the suggestion, announced instead that "Komfortabel schickt sein Pferd zurück."
3. "Aufstossen" instead of "anstossen."

4. "Begleit-digen" compounded of "begleiten" and "beleidigen."
5. "Briefkasten" instead of "Brütkasten."
6. "Geneigt" instead of "geeignet."
7. "Versuchungen" instead of "Versuche."
8. "Aufgepatzt" instead of "aufgeputzt."
9. "Angenommen" is a verb, meaning "to accept."

II

AT the last session we conceived the idea of considering the error, not in its relation to the intended act which it distorted, but by itself alone, and we received the impression that in isolated instances it seems to betray a meaning of its own. We declared that if this fact could be established on a larger scale, then the meaning of the error itself would soon come to interest us more than an investigation of the circumstances under which the error occurs.

Let us agree once more on what we understand by the "meaning" of a psychic process. A psychic process is nothing more than the purpose which it serves and the position which it holds in a psychic sequence. We can also substitute the word "purpose" or "intention" for "meaning" in most of our investigations. Was it then only a deceptive appearance or a poetic exaggeration of the importance of an error which made us believe that we recognized a purpose in it?

Let us adhere faithfully to the illustrative example of slips of the tongue and let us examine a larger number of such observations. We then find whole categories of cases in which the intention, the meaning of the slip itself, is clearly manifest. This is the case above all in those examples in which one says the opposite of what one intended. The president said, in his opening address, "I declare the meeting closed." His intention is certainly not ambiguous. The meaning and purpose of his slip is that he wants to terminate the meeting. One might point the conclusion with the remark "he said so himself." We have only taken him at his word. Do not interrupt me at this point by remarking that this is not possible, that we know he did not want to terminate the meeting but to open it, and that he himself, whom we have just recognized as the best judge of his intention, will affirm that he meant to open it. In so doing you forget that we have agreed to consider the error entirely by itself. Its relation to the intention which it distorts is to be discussed later. Otherwise you convict yourself of an error in logic by which you smoothly conjure away the problem under discussion; or "beg the question," as it is called in English.

In other cases in which the speaker has not said the exact opposite of what he intended, the slip may nevertheless express an antithetical meaning. "I am not *inclined* to appreciate the merits of my predecessor." "*Inclined*" is not the opposite of "*in a position to*," but it is an open betrayal of intent in sharpest contradiction to the attempt to cope gracefully with the situation which the speaker is supposed to meet.

In still other cases the slip simply adds a second meaning to the one intended. The sentence then sounds like a contradiction, an abbreviation, a condensation of several sentences. Thus the lady of energetic disposition, "He may eat and drink whatever *I* please." The real meaning of this abbreviation is as though the lady had said, "He may eat and drink whatever he pleases. But what does it matter what *he* pleases! It is *I* who do the pleasing." Slips of the tongue often give the impression of such an abbreviation. For example, the anatomy professor, after his lecture on the human nostril, asks whether the class has thoroughly understood, and after a unanimous answer in the affirmative, goes on to say: "I can hardly believe that is so, since the people who understand the human nostril can, even in a city of millions, be counted on *one finger*—I mean, on the fingers of one hand."

The abbreviated sentence here also has its meaning: it expresses the idea that there is only one person who thoroughly understands the subject.

In contrast to these groups of cases are those in which the error does not itself express its meaning, in which the slip of the tongue does not in itself convey anything intelligible; cases, therefore, which are in sharpest opposition to our expectations. If anyone, through a slip of the tongue, distorts a proper name, or puts together an unusual combination of syllables, then this very common occurrence seems already to have decided in the negative the question of whether all errors contain a meaning. Yet closer inspection of these examples discloses the fact that an understanding of such a distortion is easily possible, indeed, that the difference between these unintelligible cases and the previous comprehensible ones is not so very great.

A man who was asked how his horse was, answered, "Oh, it may *stake*—it may take another month." When asked what he really meant to say, he explained that he had been thinking that it was a *sorry* business and the coming together of "*take*" and "*sorry*" gave rise to "*stake*." (Meringer and Mayer.)

Another man was telling of some incidents to which he had objected, and went on, "and then certain facts were *re-filed*." Upon being questioned, he explained that he meant to stigmatize these facts as "*filthy.*" "*Revealed*" and "*filthy*" together produced the peculiar "*re-filled.*" (Meringer and Mayer.)

You will recall the case of the young man who wished to "*inscort*" an unknown lady. We took the liberty of resolving this word construction into the two words "*escort*" and "*insult*," and felt convinced of this interpretation without demanding proof of it. You see from these examples that even slips can be explained through the concurrence, the interference, of two speeches of different intentions. The difference arises only from the fact that in the one type of slip the intended speech completely crowds out the other, as happens in those slips where the opposite is said, while in the other type the intended speech must rest content with so distorting or modifying the other as to result in mixtures which seem more or less intelligible in themselves.

We believe that we have now grasped the secret of a large number of slips of the tongue. If we keep this explanation in mind we will be able to understand still other hitherto mysterious groups. In the case of the distortion of names, for instance, we cannot assume that it is always an instance of competition between two similar, yet different names. Still, the second intention is not difficult to guess. The distorting of names occurs frequently enough not as a slip of the tongue, but as an attempt to give the name an ill-sounding or debasing character. It is a familiar device or trick of insult, which persons of culture early learned to do without, though they do not give it up readily. They often clothe it in the form of a joke, though, to be sure, the joke is of a very low order. Just to cite a gross and ugly example of such a distortion of a name, I mention the fact that the name of the President of the French Republic, *Poincaré*, has been at times, lately, transformed into "*Schweinskarré*." It is therefore easy to assume that there is also such an intention to insult in the case of other slips of the tongue which result in the distortion of a name. In consequence of our adherence to this conception, similar explanations force themselves upon us, in the case of slips of the tongue whose effect is comical or absurd. "I call upon you to *hiccough* the health of our chief."[1] Here the solemn atmosphere is unexpectedly disturbed by the introduction of a word that awakens an unpleasant image; and from the prototype of certain expressions of insult and offense we cannot but suppose that there is an intention striving for expression which is in sharp contrast to the ostensible respect, and which could be expressed about as follows, "You needn't believe this. I'm not really in earnest. I don't give a whoop for the fellow—etc." A similar trick which passes for a slip of the tongue is that which transforms a harmless word into one which is indecent and obscene.[2]

We know that many persons have this tendency of intentionally making harmless words obscene for the sake of a certain lascivious pleasure it gives them. It passes as wit, and we always have to ask about a person of whom we hear such a thing, whether he intended it as a joke or whether it occurred as a slip of the tongue.

Well, here we have solved the riddle of errors with relatively little trouble! They are not accidents, but valid psychic acts. They have their meaning; they arise through the collaboration—or better, the mutual interference—of two different intentions. I can well understand that at this point you want to swamp me with a deluge of questions and doubts to be answered and resolved before we can rejoice over this first result of our labors. I truly do not wish to push you to premature conclusions. Let us dispassionately weigh each thing in turn, one after the other.

What would you like to say? Whether I think this explanation is valid for all cases of slips of the tongue or only for a certain number? Whether one can extend this same conception to all the many other errors—to mis-reading, slips of the pen, forgetting, picking up the wrong object, mislaying things, etc? In the face of the psychic nature of errors, what meaning is left to the factors of fatigue, excitement, absent-mindedness and distraction of attention? Moreover, it is easy to see that of the two competing meanings in an error, one is always public, but the other not always. But what does one do in order to guess the latter? And when one believes one has guessed it, how does one go about proving that it is not merely a probable meaning, but that it is the only correct meaning? Is there anything else you wish to ask? If not, then I will continue. I would remind you of the fact that we really are not much concerned with the errors themselves, but we wanted only to learn something of value to psychoanalysis from their study. Therefore, I put the question: What are these purposes or tendencies which can thus interfere with others, and what relation is there between the interfering tendencies and those interfered with? Thus our labor really begins anew, after the explanation of the problem.

Now, is this the explanation of all tongue slips? I am very much inclined to think so and for this reason, that as often as one investigates a case of a slip of the tongue, it reduces itself to this type of explanation. But on the other hand, one cannot prove that a slip of the tongue cannot occur without this mechanism. It may be so; for our purposes it is a matter of theoretical indifference, since the conclusions which we wish to draw by way of an introduction to psychoanalysis remain untouched, even if only a minority of the cases of tongue slips come within our conception, which is surely not the case. I shall anticipate the next question, of whether or not we may extend to other types of errors what we have gleaned from slips of the tongue, and answer it in the affirmative. You will convince yourselves of that conclusion when we turn our attention to the investigation of examples of pen slips, picking up wrong objects, etc. I would advise you, however, for technical reasons, to postpone this task until we shall have investigated the tongue slip itself more thoroughly.

The question of what meaning those factors which have been placed in the foreground by some authors,—namely, the factors of circulatory disturbances, fatigue, excitement, absent-mindedness, the theory of the distraction of attention —the question of what meaning those factors can now have for us if we accept the above described psychic mechanism of tongue slips, deserves a more detailed answer. You will note that we do not deny these factors. In fact, it is not very often that psychoanalysis denies anything which is asserted on the other side. As a rule psychoanalysis merely adds something to such assertions and occasionally it does happen that what had hitherto been overlooked, and was newly added by psychoanalysis, is just the essential thing. The influence on the occurrence of tongue slips of such physiological predispositions as result from slight illness, circulatory disturbances and conditions of fatigue, should be acknowledged without more ado. Daily personal experience can convince you of that. But how little is explained by such an admission! Above all, they are not necessary conditions of the errors. Slips of the tongue are just as possible when one is in perfect health and normal condition. Bodily factors, therefore, have only the value of acting by way of facilitation and encouragement to the peculiar psychic mechanism of a slip of the tongue.

To illustrate this relationship, I once used a simile which I will now repeat because I know of no better one as substitute. Let us suppose that some dark night I go past a lonely spot and am there assaulted by a rascal who takes my watch and purse; and then, since I did not see the face of the robber clearly, I make my complaint at the nearest police station in the following words: "Loneliness and darkness have just robbed me of my valuables." The police commissioner could then say to me: "You seem to hold an unjustifiably extreme mechanistic conception. Let us rather state the case as follows: Under cover of darkness, and favored by the loneliness, an unknown robber seized your valuables. The essential task in your case seems to me to be to discover the robber. Perhaps we can then take his booty from him again."

Such psycho-physiological moments as excitement, absent-mindedness and distracted attention, are obviously of small assistance to us for the purpose of explanation. They are mere phrases, screens behind which we will not be deterred from looking. The question is rather what in such cases has caused the excitement, the particular diversion of attention. The influence of syllable sounds, word resemblances and the customary associations which words arouse should also be recognized as having significance. They facilitate the tongue slip by pointing the path which it can take. But if I have a path before me, does that fact as a matter of course determine that I will follow it? After all, I must have a stimulus to make me decide for it, and, in addition, a force which carries me forward on this path. These sound and word relationships therefore serve also only to facilitate the tongue slip, just as the bodily dispositions facilitate them; they cannot give the explanation for the word itself. Just consider, for example, the fact that in an enormously large number of cases, my lecturing is not disturbed by the fact that the words which I use recall others by their sound resemblance, that they are intimately associated with their opposites, or arouse common associations. We might add here the observation of the philosopher Wundt, that slips of the tongue occur when, in consequence of bodily fatigue, the tendency to association gains the upper hand over the intended speech. This would sound very plausible if it were not contradicted by experiences which proved that from one series of cases of tongue-slips bodily stimuli were absent, and from another, the association stimuli were absent.

However, your next question is one of particular interest to me, namely: in what way can one establish the existence of the two mutually antagonistic tendencies? You probably do not suspect how significant this question is. It is true, is it not, that one of the two tendencies, the tendency which suffers the interference, is always unmistakable? The person who commits the error is aware of it and acknowledges it. It is the other tendency, what we call the interfering tendency, which causes doubt and hesitation. Now we have already learned, and you have surely not forgotten, that these tendencies are, in a series of cases, equally plain. That is indicated by the effect of the slip, if only we have the courage to let this effect be valid in itself. The president who said the opposite of what he meant to say made it clear that he wanted to open the meeting, but equally clear that he would also have liked to terminate it. Here the meaning is so plain that there is nothing left to be interpreted. But the other cases in which the interfering tendency merely distorts the original, without bringing itself to full expression—how can one guess the interfering meaning from the distortion?

By a very sure and simple method, in the first series of cases, namely, by the same method by which one establishes the existence of the meaning interfered with. The latter is immediately supplied by the speaker, who instantly adds the originally intended expression. "It may *stake*—no, it may *take* another month." Now we likewise ask him to express the interfering meaning; we ask him: "Now, why did you first say *stake*?" He answers, "I meant to say—'This is a *sorry* business.'" And in the other case of the tongue slip—*re-filed*—the subject also affirms that he meant to say "It is a *fil-thy* business," but then moderated his expression and turned it into something else. Thus the discovery of the interfering meaning was here as successful as the discovery of the one interfered with. Nor did I unintentionally select as examples cases which were neither related nor explained by me or by a supporter of my theories. Yet a certain investigation was necessary in both cases in order to obtain the solution. One had to ask the speaker why he made this slip, what he had to say about it. Otherwise he might perhaps have passed it by without seeking to explain it. When questioned, however, he furnished the explanation by means of the first thing that came to his mind. And now you see, ladies and gentlemen, that this slight investigation and its consequence are already a psychoanalysis, and the prototype of every psychoanalytic investigation which we shall conduct more extensively at a later time.

Now, am I unduly suspicious if I suspect that at the same moment in which psychoanalysis emerges before you, your resistance to psychoanalysis also raises its head? Are you not anxious to raise the objection that the information given by the subject we questioned, and who committed the slip, is not proof sufficient? He naturally has the desire, you say, to meet the challenge, to explain the slip, and hence he says the first thing he can think of if it seems relevant. But that, you say, is no proof that this is really the way the slip happened. It might be so, but it might just as well be otherwise, you say. Something else might have occurred to him which might have fitted the case just as well and better.

It is remarkable how little respect, at bottom, you have for a psychic fact! Imagine that someone has decided to undertake the chemical analysis of a certain substance, and has secured a sample of the substance, of a certain weight—so and so many milligrams. From this weighed sample certain definite conclusions can be drawn. Do you think it would ever occur to a chemist to discredit these conclusions by the argument that the isolated substance might have had some other weight? Everyone yields to the fact that it was just this weight and no other, and confidently builds his further conclusions upon that fact. But when you are confronted by the psychic fact that the subject, when questioned, had a certain idea, you will not accept that as valid, but say some other idea might just as easily have occurred to him! The trouble is that you believe in the illusion of psychic freedom and will not give it up. I regret that on this point I find myself in complete opposition to your views.

Now you will relinquish this point only to take up your resistance at another place. You will continue, "We understand that it is the peculiar technique of psychoanalysis that the solution of its problems is discovered by the analyzed subject himself. Let us take another example, that in which the speaker calls upon the assembly 'to *hiccough* the health of their chief.' The interfering idea in this case, you say, is the insult. It is that which is the antagonist of the expression of conferring an honor. But that is mere interpretation on your part, based on observations extraneous to the slip. If in this case you question the originator of the slip, he will not affirm that he intended an insult, on the contrary, he will deny it energetically. Why do you not give up your unverifiable interpretation in the face of this plain objection?"

Yes, this time you struck a hard problem. I can imagine the unknown speaker. He is probably an assistant to the guest of honor, perhaps already a minor official, a young man with the brightest prospects. I will press him as to whether he did not after all feel conscious of something which may have worked in opposition to the demand that he do honor to the chief. What a fine success I'll have! He becomes impatient and suddenly bursts out on me, "Look here, you'd better stop this cross-examination, or I'll get unpleasant. Why, you'll spoil my whole career with your suspicions. I simply said '*auf*-gestossen' instead of '*an*-gestossen,' because I'd already said '*auf*' twice in the same sentence. It's the thing that Meringer calls a perservation, and there's no other meaning that you can twist out of it. Do you understand me? That's all." H'm, this is a surprising reaction, a really energetic denial. I see that there is nothing more to be obtained from the young man, but I also remark to myself that he betrays a strong personal interest in having his slip mean nothing. Perhaps you, too, agree that it is not right for him immediately to become so rude over a purely theoretical investigation, but, you will conclude, he really must know what he did and did not mean to say.

Really? Perhaps that's open to question nevertheless.

But now you think you have me. "So that is your technique," I hear you say. "When the person who has committed a slip gives an explanation which fits your theory, then you declare him the final authority on the subject. 'He says so himself!' But if what he says does not fit into your scheme, then you suddenly assert that what he says does not count, that one need not believe him."

Yet that is certainly true. I can give you a similar case in which the procedure is apparently just as monstrous. When a defendant confesses to a deed, the judge believes his confession. But if he denies it, the judge does not believe him. Were it otherwise, there would be no way to administer the law, and despite occasional miscarriages you must acknowledge the value of this system.

Well, are you then the judge, and is the person who committed the slip a defendant before you? Is a slip of the tongue a crime?

Perhaps we need not even decline this comparison. But just see to what far-reaching differences we have come by penetrating somewhat into the seemingly harmless problems of the psychology of errors, differences which at this stage we do not at all know how to reconcile. I offer you a preliminary compromise on the basis of the analogy of the judge and the defendant. You will grant me that the meaning of an error admits of no doubt when the subject under analysis acknowledges it himself. I in turn will admit that a direct proof for the suspected meaning cannot be obtained if the subject denies us the information; and, of course, that is also the case when the subject is not present to give us the information. We are, then, as in the case of the legal procedure, dependent on circumstances which make a decision at one time seem more, and at another time, less probable to us. At law, one has to declare a defendant guilty on circumstantial evidence for practical reasons. We see no such necessity; but neither are we forced to forego the use of these circumstances. It would be a mistake to believe that a science consists of nothing but conclusively proved theorems, and any such demand would be unjust. Only a person with a mania for authority, a person who must replace his religious catechism with some other, even though it be scientific, would make such a demand. Science has but few apodeictic precepts in its catechism; it consists chiefly of assertions which it has developed to certain degrees of probability. It is actually a symptom of scientific thinking if one is content with these approximations of certainty and is able to carry on constructive work despite the lack of the final confirmation.

But where do we get the facts for our interpretations, the circumstances for our proof, when the further remarks of the subject under analysis do not themselves elucidate the meaning of the error? From many sources. First of all, from the analogy with phenomena extraneous to the psychology of errors; as, for example, when we assert that the distortion of a name as a slip of the tongue has the same insulting significance as an intentional name distortion. We get them also from the psychic situation in which the error occurred, from our knowledge of the character of the person who committed the error, from the impressions which that person received before making the error, and to which he may possibly have reacted with this error. As a rule, what happens is that we find the meaning of the error according to general principles. It is then only a conjecture, a suggestion as to what the meaning may be, and we then obtain our proof from examination of the psychic situation. Sometimes, too, it happens that we have to wait for subsequent developments, which have announced themselves, as it were, through the error, in order to find our conjecture verified.

I cannot easily give you proof of this if I have to limit myself to the field of tongue slips, although even here there are a few good examples. The young man who wished to "*inscort*" the lady is certainly shy; the lady whose husband may eat and drink whatever *she* wants I know to be one of those energetic women who know how to rule in the home. Or take the following case: At a general meeting of the Concordia Club, a young member delivers a vehement speech in opposition, in the course of which he addresses the officers of the society as: "Fellow committee lenders." We will conjecture that some conflicting idea militated in him against his opposition, an idea which was in some way based on a connection with money lending. As a matter of fact, we learn from our informant that the speaker was in constant money difficulties, and had attempted to raise a loan. As a conflicting idea, therefore, we may safely interpolate the idea, "Be more moderate in your opposition, these are the same people who are to grant you the loan."

But I can give you a wide selection of such circumstantial proof if I delve into the wide field of other kinds of error.

If anyone forgets an otherwise familiar proper name, or has difficulty in retaining it in his memory despite all efforts, then the conclusion lies close at hand, that he has something against the bearer of this name and does not like to think of him. Consider in this connection the following revelation of the psychic situation in which this error occurs:

"A Mr. Y. fell in love, without reciprocation, with a lady who soon after married a Mr. X. In spite of the fact that Mr. Y. has known Mr. X. a long time, and even has business relations with him, he forgets his name over and over again, so that he found it necessary on several occasions to ask other people the man's name when he wanted to write to Mr. X."[3]

Mr. Y. obviously does not want to have his fortunate rival in mind under any condition. "Let him never be thought of."

Another example: A lady makes inquiries at her doctor's concerning a mutual acquaintance, but speaks of her by her maiden name. She has forgotten her married name. She admits that she was much displeased by the marriage, and could not stand this friend's husband.[4]

Later we shall have much to say in other relations about the matter of forgetting names. At present we are predominantly interested in the psychic situation in which the lapse of memory occurs.

The forgetting of projects can quite commonly be traced to an antagonistic current which does not wish to carry out the project. We psychoanalysts are not alone in holding this view, but this is the general conception to which all persons subscribe the daily affairs, and which they first deny in theory. The patron who makes apologies to his protégé, saying that he has forgotten his requests, has not squared himself with his protégé. The protegé immediately thinks: "There's nothing to that; he did promise but he really doesn't want to do it." Hence, daily life also proscribes forgetting, in certain connections, and the difference between the popular and the psychoanalytic conception of these errors appears to be removed. Imagine a housekeeper who receives her guest with the words: "What, you come to-day? Why, I had totally forgotten that I had invited you for to-day"; or the young man who might tell his sweetheart that he had forgotten to keep the rendezvous which they planned. He is sure not to admit it, it were better for him to invent the most improbable excuses on the spur of the moment, hindrances which prevented him from coming at that time, and which made it impossible for him to communicate the situation to her. We all know that in military matters the excuse of having forgotten something is useless, that it protects one from no punishment; and we must consider this attitude justified. Here we suddenly find everyone agreed that a certain error is significant, and everyone agrees what its meaning is. Why are they not consistent enough to extend this insight to the other errors, and fully to acknowledge them? Of course, there is also an answer to this.

If the meaning of this forgetting of projects leaves room for so little doubt among laymen, you will be less surprised to find that poets make use of these errors in the same sense. Those of you who have seen or read Shaw's *Caesar and Cleopatra* will recall that Caesar, when departing in the last scene, is pursued by the idea that there was something more he intended to do, but that he had forgotten it. Finally he discovers what it is: to take leave of Cleopatra. This small device of the author is meant to ascribe to the great Caesar a superiority which he did not possess, and to which he did not at all aspire. You can learn from historical sources that Caesar had Cleopatra follow him to Rome, and that she was staying there with her little Caesarion when Caesar was murdered, whereupon she fled the city.

The cases of forgetting projects are as a rule so clear that they are of little use for our purpose, i.e., discovering in the psychic situation circumstantial evidence of the meaning of the error. Let us, therefore, turn to a particularly ambiguous and untransparent error, that of losing and mislaying objects. That we ourselves should have a purpose in losing an object, an accident frequently so painful, will certainly seem incredible to you. But there are many instances similar to the following: A young man loses the pencil which he had liked very much. The day before he had received a letter from his brother-in-law, which concluded with the words, "For the present I have neither the inclination nor the time to be a party to your frivolity and your idleness." ⁵ It so happened that the pencil had been a present from this brother-in-law. Without this coincidence we could not, of course, assert that the loss involved any intention to get rid of the gift. Similar cases are numerous. Persons lose objects when they have fallen out with the donors, and no longer wish to be reminded of them. Or again, objects may be lost if one no longer likes the things themselves, and wants to supply oneself with a pretext for substituting other and better things in their stead. Letting a thing fall and break naturally shows the same intention toward that object. Can one consider it accidental when a school child just before his birthday loses, ruins or breaks his belongings, for example his school bag or his watch?

He who has frequently experienced the annoyance of not being able to find something which he has himself put away, will also be unwilling to believe there was any intent behind the loss. And yet the examples are not at all rare in which the attendant circumstances of the mislaying point to a tendency temporarily or permanently to get rid of the object. Perhaps the most beautiful example of this sort is the following: A young man tells me: "A few years ago a misunderstanding arose in my married life. I felt my wife was too cool and even though I willingly acknowledged her excellent qualities, we lived without any tenderness between us. One day she brought me a book which she had thought might interest me. I thanked her for this attention, promised to read the book, put it in a handy place, and couldn't find it again. Several months passed thus, during which I occasionally remembered this mislaid book and tried in vain to find it. About half a year later my beloved mother, who lived at a distance from us, fell ill. My wife left the house in order to nurse her mother-in-law. The condition of the patient became serious, and gave my wife an opportunity of showing her best side. One evening I came home filled with enthusiasm and gratitude toward my wife. I approached my writing desk, opened a certain drawer with no definite intention but as if with somnambulistic certainty, and the first thing I found is the book so long mislaid."

With the cessation of the motive, the inability to find the mislaid object also came to an end.

Ladies and gentlemen, I could increase this collection of examples indefinitely. But I do not wish to do so here. In my *Psychopathology of Everyday Life* (first published in 1901), you will find only too many instances for the study of errors.[6]

All these examples demonstrate the same thing repeatedly: namely, they make it seem probable that errors have a meaning, and show how one may guess or establish that meaning from the attendant circumstances. I limit myself to-day because we have confined ourselves to the purpose of profiting in the preparation for psychoanalysis from the study of these phenomena. I must, however, still go into two additional groups of observations, into the accumulated and combined errors and into the confirmation of our interpretations by means of subsequent developments.

The accumulated and combined errors are surely the fine flower of their species. If we were interested only in proving that errors may have a meaning, we would limit ourselves to the accumulated and combined errors in the first place, for here the meaning is unmistakable, even to the dullest intelligence, and can force conviction upon the most critical judgment. The accumulation of manifestations betrays a stubbornness such as could never come about by accident, but which fits closely the idea of design. Finally, the interchange of certain kinds of error with each other shows us what is the important and essential element of the error, not its form or the means of which it avails itself, but the purpose which it serves and which is to be achieved by the most various paths. Thus I will give you a case of repeated forgetting. Jones recounts that he once allowed a letter to lie on his writing desk several days for reasons quite unknown. Finally he made up his mind to mail it; but it was returned from the dead letter office, for he had forgotten to address it. After he had addressed it he took it to the post office, but this time without a stamp. At this point he finally had to admit to himself his aversion against sending the letter at all.

In another case a mistake is combined with mislaying an object. A lady is traveling to Rome with her brother-in-law, a famous artist. The visitor is much fêted by the Germans living in Rome, and receives as a gift, among other things, a gold medal of ancient origin. The lady is vexed by the fact that her brother-in-law does not sufficiently appreciate the beautiful object. After she leaves her sister and reaches her home, she discovers when unpacking that she has brought with her—how, she does not know—the medal. She immediately informs her brother-in-law of this fact by letter, and gives him notice that she will send the medal back to Rome the next day. But on the following day, the medal has been so cleverly mislaid that it can neither be found nor sent, and at this point it begins to dawn upon the lady that her "absent-mindedness" means, namely, that she wants to keep the object for herself.[7]

I have already given you an example of a combination of forgetfulness and error in which someone first forgot a rendezvous and then, with the firm intention of not forgetting it a second time, appeared at the wrong hour. A quite analogous case was told me from his own experience, by a friend who pursues literary interests in addition to his scientific ones. He said: "A few years ago I accepted the election to the board of a certain literary society, because I hoped that the society could at some time be of use to me in helping obtain the production of my drama, and, despite my lack of interest, I took part in the meetings every Friday. A few months ago I received the assurance of a production in the theatre in F., and since that time it happens regularly that I forget the meetings of that society. When I read your article on these things, I was ashamed of my forgetfulness, reproached myself with the meanness of staying away now that I no longer need these people and determined to be sure not to forget next Friday. I kept reminding myself of this resolution until I carried it out and stood before the door of the meeting room. To my astonishment, it was closed, the meeting was already over; for I had mistaken the day. It was already Saturday."

It would be tempting enough to collect similar observations, but I will go no further; I will let you glance instead upon those cases in which our interpretation has to wait for its proof upon future developments.

The chief condition of these cases is conceivably that the existing psychic situation is unknown to us or inaccessible to our inquiries. At that time our interpretation has only the value of a conjecture to which we ourselves do not wish to grant too much weight. Later, however, something happens which shows us how justified was our interpretation even at that time. I was once the guest of a young married couple and heard the young wife laughingly tell of a recent experience, of how on the day after her return from her honeymoon she had hunted up her unmarried sister again in order to go shopping with her, as in former times, while her husband went to his business. Suddenly she noticed a gentleman on the other side of the street, and she nudged her sister, saying, "Why look, there goes Mr. K." She had forgotten that this gentleman was her husband of some weeks' standing. I shuddered at this tale but did not dare to draw the inference. The little anecdote did not occur to me again until a year later, after this marriage had come to a most unhappy end.

A. Maeder tells of a lady who, the day before her wedding, forgot to try on her wedding dress and to the despair of the dressmaker only remembered it later in the evening. He adds in connection with this forgetfulness the fact that she divorced her husband soon after. I know a lady now divorced from her husband, who, in managing her fortune, frequently signed documents with her maiden name, and this many years before she really resumed it. I know of other women who lost their wedding rings on their honeymoon and also know that the course of the marriage gave a meaning to this accident. And now one more striking example with a better termination. It is said that the marriage of a famous German chemist did not take place because he forgot the hour of the wedding, and instead of going to the church went to the laboratory. He was wise enough to rest satisfied with this one attempt, and died unmarried at a ripe old age.

Perhaps the idea has also come to you that in these cases mistakes have taken the place of the *Omina* or omens of the ancients. Some of the *Omina* really were nothing more than mistakes; for example, when a person stumbled or fell down. Others, to be sure, bore the characteristics of objective occurrences rather than that of subjective acts. But you would not believe how difficult it sometimes is to decide in a specific instance whether the act belongs to the one or the other group. It so frequently knows how to masquerade as a passive experience.

Everyone of us who can look back over a longer or shorter life experience will probably say that he might have spared himself many disappointments and painful surprises if he had found the courage and decision to interpret as omens the little mistakes which he made in his intercourse with people, and to consider them as indications of the intentions which were still being kept secret. As a rule, one does not dare do this. One would feel as though he were again becoming superstitious via a detour through science. But not all omens come true, and you will understand from our theories that they need not all come true.

---

1. The young man here said "aufzustossen" instead of "anzustossen."
2. Prof. Freud here gives the two examples, quite untranslatable, of "apopos" instead of "apropos," and "eischeiszwaibehen" instead of "eiweiszscheibehen."
3. From C. G. Jung.
4. From A. A. Brill.
5. From B. Dattner.
6. So also in the writings of A. Maeder (French), A. A. Brill (English) J. Stärke (Dutch) and others.
7. From R. Reitler.

III

WE may certainly put it down as the conclusion of our labors up to this point that errors have a meaning, and we may make this conclusion the basis of our further investigations. Let me stress the fact once more that we do not assert—and for our purposes need not assert—that every single mistake which occurs is meaningful, although I consider that probable. It will suffice us if we prove the presence of such a meaning with relative frequency in the various forms of errors. These various forms, by the way, behave differently in this respect. In the cases of tongue slips, pen slips, etc., the occurrences may take place on a purely physiological basis. In the group based on forgetfulness (forgetting names or projects, mislaying objects, etc.) I cannot believe in such a basis. There does very probably exist a type of case in which the loss of objects should be recognized as unintentional. Of the mistakes which occur in daily life, only a certain portion can in any way be brought within our conception. You must keep this limitation in mind when we start henceforth from the assumption that mistakes are psychic acts and arise through the mutual interference of two intentions.

Herein we have the first result of psychoanalysis. Psychology hitherto knew nothing of the occurrence of such interferences and the possibility that they might have such manifestations as a consequence. We have widened the province of the world of psychic phenomena quite considerably, and have brought into the province of psychology phenomena which formerly were not attributed to it.

Let us tarry a moment longer over the assertion that errors are psychic acts. Does such an assertion contain more than the former declaration that they have a meaning? I do not believe so. On the contrary, it is rather more indefinite and open to greater misunderstanding. Everything which can be observed about the psychic life will on occasion be designated as a psychic phenomenon. But it will depend on whether the specific psychic manifestations resulted directly from bodily, organic, material influences, in which case their investigation will not fall within the province of psychology, or whether it was more immediately the result of other psychic occurrences back of which, somewhere, the series of organic influences then begins. We have the latter condition of affairs before us when we designate a phenomenon as a psychic manifestation, and for that reason it is more expedient to put our assertion in this form: the phenomena are meaningful; they have a meaning. By "meaning" we understand significance, purpose, tendency and position in a sequence of psychic relations.

There are a number of other occurrences which are very closely related to errors, but which this particular name no longer fits. We call them *accidental and symptomatic* acts. They also have the appearance of being unmotivated, the appearance of insignificance and unimportance, but in addition, and more plainly, of superfluity. They are differentiated from errors by the absence of another intention with which they collide and by which they are disturbed. On the other side they pass over without a definite boundary line into the gestures and movements which we count among expressions of the emotions. Among these accidental acts belong all those apparently playful, apparently purposeless performances in connection with our clothing, parts of our body, objects within reach, as well as the omission of such performances, and the melodies which we hum to ourselves. I venture the assertion that all these phenomena are meaningful and capable of interpretation in the same way as are the errors, that they are small manifestations of other more important psychic processes, valid psychic acts. But I do not intend to linger over this new enlargement of the province of psychic phenomena, but rather to return to the topic of errors, in the consideration of which the important psychoanalytic inquiries can be worked out with far greater clarity.

The most interesting questions which we formulated while considering errors, and which we have not yet answered, are, I presume, the following: We said that the errors are the result of the mutual interference of two different intentions, of which the one can be called the intention interfered with, and the other the interfering intention. The intentions interfered with give rise to no further questions, but concerning the others we want to know, firstly, what kind of intentions are these which arise as disturbers of others, and secondly, in what proportions are the interfering related to the interfered?

Will you permit me again to take the slip of the tongue as representative of the whole species and allow me to answer the second question before the first?

The interfering intention in the tongue slip may stand in a significant relation to the intention interfered with, and then the former contains a contradiction of the latter, correcting or supplementing it. Or, to take a less intelligible and more interesting case, the interfering intention has nothing to do with the intention interfered with.

Proofs for the first of the two relations we can find without trouble in the examples which we already know and in others similar to those. In almost all cases of tongue slips where one says the contrary of what he intended, where the interfering intention expresses the antithesis of the intention interfered with, the error is the presentation of the conflict between two irreconcilable strivings. "I declare the meeting opened, but would rather have it closed," is the meaning of the president's slip. A political paper which has been accused of corruptibility, defends itself in an article meant to reach a climax in the words: "Our readers will testify that we have always interceded for the good of all in the most *disinterested* manner." But the editor who had been entrusted with the composition of the defence, wrote, "in the most *interested* manner." That is, he thinks "To be sure, I have to write this way, but I know better."

A representative of the people who urges that the Kaiser should be told the truth "*rückhaltlos*," hears an inner voice which is frightened by his boldness, and which through a slip changes the "*rückhaltlos*" into "*rückgratlos*."[1]

In the examples familiar to you, which give the impression of contraction and abbreviation, it is a question of a correction, an addition or continuation by which the second tendency manifests itself together with the first. "Things were revealed, but better say it right out, they were *filthy*, therefore, things were *refiled*."[2] "The people who understand this topic can be counted on the *fingers of one hand*, but no, there is really only *one* who understands it; therefore, counted *on one finger*." Or, "My husband may eat and drink whatever *he* wants. But you know very well that *I* don't permit him to want anything; therefore he may eat and drink whatever *I want*." In all these cases, therefore, the slip arises from the content of the intention itself, or is connected with it.

The other type of relationship between the two interfering intentions seems strange. If the interfering intention has nothing to do with the content of the one interfered with, where then does it come from and how does it happen to make itself manifest as interference just at that point? The observation which alone can furnish an answer here, recognizes the fact that the interference originates in a thought process which has just previously occupied the person in question and which then has that after-effect, irrespective of whether it has already found expression in speech or not. It is therefore really to be designated as perseveration, but not necessarily as the perseveration of spoken words. Here also there is no lack of an associative connection between the interfering and the interfered with, yet it is not given in the content, but artificially restored, often by means of forced connecting links.

Here is a simple example of this, which I myself observed. In our beautiful Dolomites, I meet two Viennese ladies who are gotten up as tourists. I accompany them a short distance and we discuss the pleasures, but also the difficulties of the tourist's mode of life. One lady admits this way of spending the day entails much discomfort. "It is true," she says, "that it is not at all pleasant, when one has tramped all day in the sun, and waist and shirt are soaked through." At this point in this sentence she suddenly has to overcome a slight hesitancy. Then she continues: "But then, when one gets *nach Hose*, and can change...."[3] We did not analyze this slip, but I am sure you can easily understand it. The lady wanted to make the enumeration more complete and to say, "Waist, shirt and drawers." From motives of propriety, the mention of the drawers (Hose) was suppressed, but in the next sentence of quite independent content the unuttered word came to light as a distortion of the similar word, house (Hause).

Now we can turn at last to the long delayed main question, namely, what kind of intentions are these which get themselves expressed in an unusual way as interferences of others, intentions within whose great variety we wish nevertheless to find what is common to them all! If we examine a series of them to this end, we will soon find that they divide themselves into three groups. In the first group belong the cases in which the interfering tendency is known to the speaker, and which, moreover, was felt by him before the slip. Thus, in the case of the slip *"refilled,"* the speaker not only admits that he agreed with the judgment *"filthy,"* on the incidents in question, but also that he had the intention (which he later abandoned) of giving it verbal expression. A second group is made up of those cases in which the interfering tendency is immediately recognized by the subject as his own, but in which he is ignorant of the fact that the interfering tendency was active in him just before the slip. He therefore accepts our interpretation, yet remains to a certain extent surprised by it. Examples of this situation can perhaps more easily be found among errors other than slips of the tongue. In a third group the interpretation of the interfering intention is energetically denied by the speaker. He not only denies that the interfering tendency was active in him before the slip, but he wants to assert that it was at all times completely alien to him. Will you recall the example of "hiccough," and the absolutely impolite disavowal which I received at the hands of this speaker by my disclosure of the interfering intention. You know that so far we have no unity in our conception of these cases. I pay no attention to the toastmaster's disavowal and hold fast to my interpretation; while you, I am sure, are yet under the influence of his repudiation and are considering whether one ought not to forego the interpretation of such slips, and let them pass as purely physiological acts, incapable of further analysis. I can imagine what it is that frightens you off. My interpretation draws the conclusion that intentions of which he himself knows nothing may manifest themselves in a speaker, and that I can deduce them from the circumstances. You hesitate before so novel a conclusion and one so full of consequences. I understand that, and sympathize with you to that extent. But let us make one thing clear: if you want consistently to carry through the conception of errors which you have derived from so many examples, you must decide to accept the above conclusion, even though it be unpleasant. If you cannot do so, you must give up that understanding of errors which you have so recently won.

Let us tarry a while over the point which unites the three groups, which is common to the three mechanisms of tongue slips. Fortunately, that is unmistakable. In the first two groups the interfering tendency is recognized by the speaker; in the first there is the additional fact that it showed itself immediately before the slip. In both cases, however, *it was suppressed. The speaker had made up his mind not to convert the interfering tendency into speech and then the slip of the tongue occurred; that is to say, the suppressed tendency obtains expression against the speaker's will, in that it changes the expression of the intention which he permits, mixes itself with it or actually puts itself in its place.* This is, then, the mechanism of the tongue slip.

From my point of view, I can also best harmonize the processes of the third group with the mechanism here described. I need only assume that these three groups are differentiated by the different degrees of effectiveness attending the suppression of an intention. In the first group, the intention is present and makes itself perceptible before the utterance of the speaker; not until then does it suffer the suppression for which it indemnifies itself in the slip. In the second group the suppression extends farther. The intention is no longer perceptible before the subject speaks. It is remarkable that the interfering intention is in no way deterred by this from taking part in the causation of the slip. Through this fact, however, the explanation of the procedure in the third group is simplified for us. I shall be so bold as to assume that in the error a tendency can manifest itself which has been suppressed for even a longer time, perhaps a very long time, which does not become perceptible and which, therefore, cannot be directly denied by the speaker. But leave the problem of the third group; from the observation of the other cases, you most draw the conclusion that *the suppression of the existing intention to say something is the indispensable condition of the occurrence of a slip.*

We may now claim that we have made further progress in understanding errors. We know not only that they are psychic acts, in which we can recognize meaning and purpose, and that they arise through the mutual interference of two different intentions, but, in addition, we know that one of these intentions must have undergone a certain suppression in order to be able to manifest itself through interference with the other. The interfering intention must itself first be interfered with before it can become interfering. Naturally, a complete explanation of the phenomena which we call errors is not attained to by this. We immediately see further questions arising, and suspect in general that there will be more occasions for new questions as we progress further. We might, for example, ask why the matter does not proceed much more simply. If there is an existing purpose to suppress a certain tendency instead of giving it expression, then this suppression should be so successful that nothing at all of the latter comes to light; or it could even fail, so that the suppressed tendency attains to full expression. But errors are compromise formations. They mean some success and some failure for each of the two purposes. The endangered intention is neither completely suppressed nor does it, without regard to individual cases, come through wholly intact. We can imagine that special conditions must be existent for the occurrence of such interference or compromise formations, but then we cannot even conjecture what sort they may be. Nor do I believe that we can uncover these unknown circumstances through further penetration into the study of errors. Rather will it be necessary thoroughly to examine other obscure fields of psychic life. Only the analogies which we there encounter can give us the courage to draw those assumptions which are requisite to a more fundamental elucidation of errors. And one thing more. Even working with small signs, as we have constantly been in the habit of doing in this province, brings its dangers with it. There is a mental disease, combined paranoia, in which the utilization of such small signs is practiced without restriction and I naturally would not wish to give it as my opinion that these conclusions, built up on this basis, are correct throughout. We can be protected from such dangers only by the broad basis of our observations, by the repetition of similar impressions from the most varied fields of psychic life.

We will therefore leave the analysis of errors here. But may I remind you of one thing more: keep in mind, as a prototype, the manner in which we have treated these phenomena. You can see from these examples what the purposes of our psychology are. We do not wish merely to describe the phenomena and to classify them, but to comprehend them as signs of a play of forces in the psychic, as expressions of tendencies striving to an end, tendencies which work together or against one another. We seek a dynamic conception of psychic phenomena. The perceived phenomena must, in our conception, give way to those strivings whose existence is only assumed.

Hence we will not go deeper into the problem of errors, but we can still undertake an expedition through the length of this field, in which we will reëncounter things familiar to us, and will come upon the tracks of some that are new. In so doing we will keep to the division which we made in the beginning of our study, of the three groups of tongue slips, with the related forms of pen slips, misreadings, mishearings, forgetfulness with its subdivisions according to the forgotten object (proper names, foreign words, projects, impressions), and the other faults of mistaking, mislaying and losing objects. Errors, in so far as they come into our consideration, are grouped in part with forgetfulness, in part with mistakes.

We have already spoken in such detail of tongue slips, and yet there are still several points to be added. Linked with tongue slips are smaller effective phenomena which are not entirely without interest. No one likes to make a slip of the tongue; often one fails to hear his own slip, though never that of another. Tongue slips are in a certain sense infectious; it is not at all easy to discuss tongue slips without falling into slips of the tongue oneself. The most trifling forms of tongue slips are just the ones which have no particular illumination to throw on the hidden psychic processes, but are nevertheless not difficult to penetrate in their motivation. If, for example, anyone pronounces a long vowel as a short, in consequence of an interference no matter how motivated, he will for that reason soon after lengthen a short vowel and commit a new slip in compensation for the earlier one. The same thing occurs when one has pronounced a double vowel unclearly and hastily; for example, an "eu" or an "oi" as "ei." The speaker tries to correct it by changing a subsequent "ei" or "eu" to "oi." In this conduct the determining factor seems to be a certain consideration for the hearer, who is not to think that it is immaterial to the speaker how he treats his mother tongue. The second, compensating distortion actually has the purpose of making the hearer conscious of the first, and of assuring him that it also did not escape the speaker. The most frequent and most trifling cases of slips consist in the contractions and foresoundings which show themselves in inconspicuous parts of speech. One's tongue slips in a longer speech to such an extent that the last word of the intended speech is said too soon. That gives the impression of a certain impatience to be finished with the sentence and gives proof in general of a certain resistance to communicating this sentence or speech as a whole. Thus we come to borderline cases in which the differences between the psychoanalytic and the common physiological conception of tongue slips are blended. We assume that in these cases there is a tendency which interferes with the intention of the speech. But it can only announce that it is present, and not what its own intention is. The interference which it occasions then follows some sound influences or associative relationship, and may be considered as a distraction of attention from the intended speech. But neither this disturbance of attention nor the associative tendency which has been activated, strikes the essence of the process. This hints, however, at the existence of an intention which interferes with the purposed speech, an intention whose nature cannot (as is possible in all the more pronounced cases of tongue slips) this time be guessed from its effects.

Slips of the pen, to which I now turn, are in agreement with those of the tongue to the extent that we need expect to gain no new points of view from them. Perhaps we will be content with a small gleaning. Those very common little slips of the pen—contractions, anticipations of later words, particularly of the last words—again point to a general distaste for writing, and to an impatience to be done; the pronounced effects of pen slips permit the nature and purpose of the interfering tendency to be recognized. One knows in general that if one finds a slip of the pen in a letter everything was not as usual with the writer. What was the matter one cannot always establish. The pen slip is frequently as little noticed by the person who makes it as the tongue slip. The following observation is striking: There are some persons who have the habit of always rereading a letter they have written before sending it. Others do not do so. But if the latter make an exception and reread the letter, they always have the opportunity of finding and correcting a conspicuous pen slip. How can that be explained? This looks as if these persons knew that they had made a slip of the pen while writing the letter. Shall we really believe that such is the case?

There is an interesting problem linked with the practical significance of the pen slip. You may recall the case of the murderer H., who made a practice of obtaining cultures of the most dangerous disease germs from scientific institutions, by pretending to be a bacteriologist, and who used these cultures to get his close relatives out of the way in this most modern fashion. This man once complained to the authorities of such an institution about the ineffectiveness of the culture which had been sent to him, but committed a pen slip and instead of the words, "in my attempts on mice and guinea pigs," was plainly written, "in my attempts on people."[4] This slip even attracted the attention of the doctors at the institution, but so far as I know, they drew no conclusion from it. Now what do you think? Might not the doctors better have accepted the slip as a confession and instituted an investigation through which the murderer's handiwork would have been blocked in time? In this case was not ignorance of our conception of errors to blame for an omission of practical importance?

Well, I am inclined to think that such a slip would surely seem very suspicious to me, but a fact of great importance stands in the way of its utilization as a confession. The thing is not so simple. The pen slip is surely an indication, but by itself it would not have been sufficient to instigate an investigation. That the man is preoccupied with the thought of infecting human beings, the slip certainly does betray, but it does not make it possible to decide whether this thought has the value of a clear plan of injury or merely of a phantasy having no practical consequence. It is even possible that the person who made such a slip will deny this phantasy with the best subjective justification and will reject it as something entirely alien to him. Later, when we give our attention to the difference between psychic and material reality, you will understand these possibilities even better. Yet this is again a case in which an error later attained unsuspected significance.

In misreading, we encounter a psychic situation which is clearly differentiated from that of the tongue slips or pen slips. The one of the two rival tendencies is here replaced by a sensory stimulus and perhaps for that reason is less resistant. What one is reading is not a production of one's own psychic activity, as is something which one intends to write. In a large majority of cases, therefore, the misreading consists in a complete substitution. One substitutes another word for the word to be read, and there need be no connection in meaning between the text and the product of the misreading. In general, the slip is based upon a word resemblance. Lichtenberg's example of reading "*Agamemnon*" for "*angenommen*"[5] is the best of this group. If one wishes to discover the interfering tendency which causes the misreading, one may completely ignore the misread text and can begin the analytic investigation with the two questions: What is the first idea that occurs in free association to the product of the misreading, and, in what situation did the misreading occur? Now and then a knowledge of the latter suffices by itself to explain the misreading. Take, for example, the individual who, distressed by certain needs, wanders about in a strange city and reads the word "*Closethaus*" on a large sign on the first floor of a house. He has just time to be surprised at the fact that the sign has been nailed so high up when he discovers that, accurately observed, the sign reads "*Corset-haus*." In other cases the misreadings which are independent of the text require a penetrating analysis which cannot be accomplished without practice and confidence in the psychoanalytic technique. But generally it is not a matter of much difficulty to obtain the elucidation of a misreading. The substituted word, as in the example, "*Agamemnon*," betrays without more ado the thought sequence from which the interference results. In war times, for instance, it is very common for one to read into everything which contains a similar word structure, the names of the cities, generals and military expressions which are constantly buzzing around us. In this way, whatever interests and preoccupies one puts itself in the place of that which is foreign or uninteresting. The after-effects of thoughts blur the new perceptions.

There are other types of misreadings, in which the text itself arouses the disturbing tendency, by means of which it is then most often changed into its opposite. One reads something which is undesired; analysis then convinces one that an intensive wish to reject what has been read should be made responsible for the alteration.

In the first mentioned and more frequent cases of misreading, two factors are neglected to which we gave an important role in the mechanism of errors: the conflict of two tendencies and the suppression of one which then indemnifies itself by producing the error. Not that anything like the opposite occurs in misreading, but the importunity of the idea content which leads to misreading is nevertheless much more conspicuous than the suppression to which the latter may previously have been subjected. Just these two factors are most tangibly apparent in the various situations of errors of forgetfulness.

Forgetting plans is actually uniform in meaning; its interpretation is, as we have heard, not denied even by the layman. The tendency interfering with the plan is always an antithetical intention, an unwillingness concerning which we need only discover why it does not come to expression in a different and less disguised manner. But the existence of this unwillingness is not to be doubted. Sometimes it is possible even to guess something of the motives which make it necessary for this unwillingness to disguise itself, and it always achieves its purpose by the error resulting from the concealment, while its rejection would be certain were it to present itself as open contradiction. If an important change in the psychic situation occurs between the formulation of the plan and its execution, in consequence of which the execution of the plan does not come into question, then the fact that the plan was forgotten is no longer in the class of errors. One is no longer surprised at it, and one understands that it would have been superfluous to have remembered the plan; it was then permanently or temporarily effaced. Forgetting a plan can be called an error only when we have no reason to believe there was such an interruption.

The cases of forgetting plans are in general so uniform and transparent that they do not interest us in our investigation. There are two points, however, from which we can learn something new. We have said that forgetting, that is, the non-execution of a plan, points to an antipathy toward it. This certainly holds, but, according to the results of our investigations, the antipathy may be of two sorts, direct and indirect. What is meant by the latter can best be explained by one or two examples. If a patron forgets to say a good word for his protegé to a third person, it may be because the patron is not really very much interested in the protegé, therefore, has no great inclination to commend him. It is, at any rate, in this sense that the protegé will construe his patron's forgetfulness. But the matter may be more complicated. The patron's antipathy to the execution of the plan may originate in another quarter and fasten upon quite a different point. It need not have anything to do with the protegé, but may be directed toward the third person to whom the good word was to have been said. Thus, you see what doubts here confront the practical application of our interpretation. The protegé, despite a correct interpretation of the forgetfulness, stands in danger of becoming too suspicious, and of doing his patron a grave injustice. Or, if an individual forgets a rendezvous which he has made, and which he had resolved to keep, the most frequent basis will certainly be the direct aversion to encountering this person. But analysis might here supply the information that the interfering intention was not directed against that person, but against the place in which they were to have met, and which was avoided because of a painful memory associated with it. Or, if one forgets to mail a letter, the counter-intention may be directed against the content of that letter, yet this does not in any way exclude the possibility that the letter is harmless in itself, and only subject to the counter-intention because something about it reminds the writer of another letter written previously, which, in fact, did afford a basis for the antipathy. One can say in such a case that the antipathy has here transferred itself from that former letter where it was justified to the present one in which it really has no meaning. Thus you see that one must always exercise restraint and caution in the application of interpretations, even though the interpretations are justified. That which is psychologically equivalent may nevertheless in practice be very ambiguous.

Phenomena such as these will seem very unusual to you. Perhaps you are inclined to assume that the "indirect" antipathy is enough to characterize the incident as pathological. Yet I can assure you that it also occurs in a normal and healthy setting. I am in no way willing to admit the unreliability of our analytic interpretation. After all, the above-discussed ambiguity of plan-forgetting exists only so long as we have not attempted an analysis of the case, and are interpreting it only on the basis of our general suppositions. When we analyze the person in question, we discover with sufficient certainty in each case whether or not it is a direct antipathy, or what its origin is otherwise.

A second point is the following: when we find in a large majority of cases that the forgetting of a plan goes back to an antipathy, we gain courage to extend this solution to another series of cases in which the analyzed person does not confirm, but denies, the antipathy which we inferred. Take as an example the exceedingly frequent incidents of forgetting to return books which one has borrowed, or forgetting to pay one's bills or debts. We will be so bold as to accuse the individual in question of intending to keep the books and not to pay the debts, while he will deny such an intention but will not be in a position to give us any other explanation of his conduct. Thereupon we insist that he has the intention, only he knows nothing about it; all we need for our inference is to have the intention betray itself through the effect of the forgetfulness. The subject may then repeat that he had merely forgotten it. You now recognize the situation as one in which we once before found ourselves. If we wish to be consistent in our interpretation, an interpretation which has been proved as manifold as it is justified, we will be unavoidably forced to the conclusion that there are tendencies in a human being which can become effective without his being conscious of them. By so doing, however, we place ourselves in opposition to all the views which prevail in daily life and in psychology.

Forgetting proper names and foreign names as well as foreign words can be traced in the same manner to a counter-intention which aims either directly or indirectly at the name in question. I have already given you an example of such direct antipathy. The indirect causation, however, is particularly frequent and generally necessitates careful analysis for its determination. Thus, for example, in war times which force us to sacrifice so many of our former inclinations, the ability to recall proper names also suffers severely in consequence of the most peculiar connections. A short time ago it happened that I could not reproduce the name of that harmless Moravian city of Bisenz, and analysis showed that no direct dislike was to blame, but rather the sound resemblance to the name of the Bisenzi palace in Orrieto, in which I used to wish I might live. As a motive for the antagonism to remembering the name, we here encounter for the first time a principle which will later disclose to us its whole tremendous significance in the causation of neurotic symptoms, viz., the aversion on the part of the memory to remembering anything which is connected with unpleasant experience and which would revive this unpleasantness by a reproduction. This intention of avoiding unpleasantness in recollections of other psychic acts, the psychic flight from unpleasantness, we may recognize as the ultimate effective motive not only for the forgetting of names, but also for many other errors, such as omissions of action, etc.

Forgetting names does, however, seem to be especially facilitated psycho-physiologically and therefore also occurs in cases in which the interference of an unpleasantness-motive cannot be established. If anyone once has a tendency to forget names, you can establish by analytical investigation that he not only loses names because he himself does not like them, or because they remind him of something he does not like, but also because the same name in his mind belongs to another chain of associations, with which he has more intimate relations. The name is anchored there, as it were, and denied to the other associations activated at the moment. If you will recall the tricks of mnemonic technique you will ascertain with some surprise that one forgets names in consequence of the same associations which one otherwise purposely forms in order to save them from being forgotten. The most conspicuous example of this is afforded by proper names of persons, which conceivably enough must have very different psychic values for different people. For example, take a first name, such as Theodore. To one of you it will mean nothing special, to another it means the name of his father, brother, friend, or his own name. Analytic experience will then show you that the first person is not in danger of forgetting that a certain stranger bears this name, while the latter will be constantly inclined to withhold from the stranger this name which seems reserved for intimate relationships. Let us now assume that this associative inhibition can come into contact with the operation of the unpleasantness-principle, and in addition with an indirect mechanism, and you will be in a position to form a correct picture of the complexity of causation of this temporary name-forgetting. An adequate analysis that does justice to the facts, however, will completely disclose these complications.

Forgetting impressions and experiences shows the working of the tendency to keep unpleasantness from recollection much more clearly and conclusively than does the forgetting of names. It does not, of course, belong in its entirety to the category of errors, but only in so far as it seems to us conspicuous and unjustified, measured by the measuring stick of our accustomed conception—thus, for example, where the forgetfulness strikes fresh or important impressions or impressions whose loss tears a hole in the otherwise well-remembered sequence. Why and how it is in general that we forget, particularly why and how we forget experiences which have surely left the deepest impressions, such as the incidents of our first years of childhood, is quite a different problem, in which the defense against unpleasant associations plays a certain role but is far from explaining everything. That unpleasant impressions are easily forgotten is an indubitable fact. Various psychologists have observed it, and the great Darwin was so struck by it that he made the "golden rule" for himself of writing down with particular care observations which seemed unfavorable to his theory, since he had convinced himself that they were just the ones which would not stick in his memory.

Those who hear for the first time of this principle of defense against unpleasant recollections by means of forgetting, seldom fail to raise the objection that they, on the contrary, have had the experience that just the painful is hard to forget, inasmuch as it always comes back to mind to torture the person against his will—as, for example, the recollection of an insult or humiliation. This fact is also correct, but the objection is not valid. It is important that one begin betimes to reckon with the fact that the psychic life is the arena of the struggles and exercises of antagonistic tendencies, or, to express it in non-dynamic terminology, that it consists of contradictions and paired antagonisms. Information concerning one specific tendency is of no avail for the exclusion of its opposite; there is room for both of them. It depends only on how the opposites react upon each other, what effects will proceed from the one and what from the other.

Losing and mislaying objects is of especial interest to us because of the ambiguity and the multiplicity of tendencies in whose services the errors may act. The common element in all cases is this, that one wished to lose something. The reasons and purposes thereof vary. One loses an object when it has become damaged, when one intends to replace it with a better one, when one has ceased to like it, when it came from a person whose relations to one have become strained, or when it was obtained under circumstances of which one no longer wishes to think. The same purpose may be served by letting the object fall, be damaged or broken. In the life of society it is said to have been found that unwelcome and illegitimate children are much more often frail than those born in wedlock. To reach this result we do not need the coarse technique of the so-called angel-maker. A certain remissness in the care of the child is said to suffice amply. In the preservation of objects, the case might easily be the same as with the children.

But things may be singled out for loss without their having forfeited any of their value, namely, when there exists the intention to sacrifice something to fate in order to ward off some other dreaded loss. Such exorcisings of fate are, according to the findings of analysis, still very frequent among us; therefore, the loss of things is often a voluntary sacrifice. In the same way losing may serve the purposes of obstinacy or self-punishment. In short, the more distant motivation of the tendency to get rid of a thing oneself by means of losing it is not overlooked.

Mistakes, like other errors, are often used to fulfill wishes which one ought to deny oneself. The purpose is thus masked as fortunate accident; for instance, one of our friends once took the train to make a call in the suburbs, despite the clearest antipathy to so doing, and then, in changing cars, made the mistake of getting into the train which took him back to the city. Or, if on a trip one absolutely wants to make a longer stay at a half-way station, one is apt to overlook or miss certain connections, so that he is forced to make the desired interruption to the trip. Or, as once happened to a patient of mine whom I had forbidden to call up his fiancée on the telephone, "by mistake" and "absent-mindedly" he asked for a wrong number when he wanted to telephone to me, so that he was suddenly connected with the lady. A pretty example and one of practical significance in making a direct mistake is the observation of an engineer at a preliminary hearing in a damage suit:

"Some time ago I worked with several colleagues in the laboratory of a high school on a series of complicated elasticity experiments, a piece of work which we had undertaken voluntarily but which began to take more time than we had expected. One day as I went into the laboratory with my colleague F., the latter remarked how unpleasant it was to him to lose so much time that day, since he had so much to do at home. I could not help agreeing with him, and remarked half jokingly, alluding to an incident of the previous week: 'Let's hope that the machine gives out again so that we can stop work and go home early.'

"In the division of labor it happened that F. was given the regulation of the valve of the press, that is to say, he was, by means of a cautious opening of the valve, to let the liquid pressure from the accumulator flow slowly into the cylinder of the hydraulic press. The man who was directing the job stood by the manometer (pressure gauge) and when the right pressure had been reached called out in a loud voice: 'Stop.' At this command F. seized the valve and turned with all his might—to the left! (All valves, without exception, close to the right.) Thereby the whole pressure of the accumulator suddenly became effective in the press, a strain for which the connecting pipes are not designed, so that a connecting pipe immediately burst—quite a harmless defect, but one which nevertheless forced us to drop work for the day and go home.

"It is characteristic, by the way, that some time afterward when we were discussing this occurrence, my friend F. had no recollection whatever of my remark, which I could recall with certainty."

From this point you may reach the conjecture that it is not harmless accident which makes the hands of your domestics such dangerous enemies to your household property. But you can also raise the question whether it is always an accident when one damages himself and exposes his own person to danger. There are interests the value of which you will presently be able to test by means of the analysis of observations.

Ladies and gentlemen, this is far from being all that might be said about errors. There is indeed much left to investigate and to discuss. But I am satisfied if, from our investigations to date, your previous views are somewhat shaken and if you have acquired a certain degree of liberality in the acceptance of new ones. For the rest, I must content myself with leaving you face to face with an unclear condition of affairs. We cannot prove all our axioms by the study of errors and, indeed, are by no means solely dependent on this material. The great value of errors for our purpose lies in the fact that they are very frequent phenomena that can easily be observed on oneself and the occurrence of which do not require a pathological condition. I should like to mention just one more of your unanswered questions before concluding: "If, as we have seen in many examples, people come so close to understanding errors and so often act as though they penetrated their meaning, how is it possible that they can so generally consider them accidental, senseless and meaningless, and can so energetically oppose their psychoanalytic elucidation?"

You are right; that is conspicuous and demands an explanation. I shall not give this explanation to you, however, but shall guide you slowly to the connecting links from which the explanation will force itself upon you without any aid from me.

---

1. In the German Reichstag, November, 1908. "Rückhaltlos" means "unreservedly." "Rückgratlos" means "without backbone."
2. "Zum Vorschein bringen," means to bring to light. "Schweinereien" means filthiness or obscurity. The telescoping of the two ideas, resulting in the word

"Vorschwein," plainly reveals the speaker's opinion of the affair.
3. The lady meant to say "Nach Hause," "to reach home." The word "Hose" means "drawers." The preservating content of her hesitancy is hereby revealed.
4. The German reads, "bei meinen Versuchen an Mausen," which, through the slip of the pen, resulted in "bei meinen Versuchen an Menschen."
5. "Angenommen" is a verb, meaning "to accept."

Copyright © 2021 by FV Editions
Cover Design : Canva.com
Ebook ISBN : 9791029913310
Paperback ISBN : 9791029913327
All rights reserved.

www.ingramcontent.com/pod-product-compliance
Lightning Source LLC
LaVergne TN
LVHW030344070526
838199LV00067B/6441